REIKI FOR BEGINNERS

How to Heal Yourself with Reiki

by Brooke Betts

Reiki Master Teacher

DISCLAIMER

Reiki is an ancient Japanese healing technique, and healing and Western medicine are two very different disciplines. None of the information in this book is intended as a substitute for medical advice. If you have a serious health condition, please consult a doctor or appropriate professional.

Reproducing this book or any portion thereof without express written consent is strictly prohibited.

Table of Contents

WHY I WROTE THIS BOOK

Kindle the light in yourself, then kindle it in others,
one by one. - Babaji

O nce in a while, not every day because then it wouldn't be as special, but every now and then you receive a gift of wisdom. Perhaps this gift sneaks up on you, stemming from personal experiences that gradually alter your very perception of the world. Or maybe it hits you like a lightning bolt, offering clarity and understanding all in one fell swoop and instantly changing your life forevermore.

For me, Reiki has been a little bit of both.

This beautiful Japanese healing art has improved my life in so many ways. These days, I feel more at peace with myself, am so excited to start each day and remain committed to developing my full potential as a human being.

That's not to say I didn't go through the detoxification process that typically follows a Reiki attunement. I've definitely had my share of bumps along the way, obstacles put there not to block me but rather to teach me how to navigate my path successfully and live a life I am proud of.

But, ah, the rewards of being attuned to Reiki and having this spiritual energy flow through you.

For once you receive a Reiki attunement, your whole world changes. You have no choice but to grow. Situations you may have tolerated before - like an unfulfilling job, a relationship you've outgrown, or a life you where you just exist as a human doing instead of a human being - all these become intolerable. No longer can you try to convince yourself that you're happy if deep down your heart knows the truth.

After a Reiki attunement, you even get to the point where you say, "Bring it on. Bring on the uncertainty, the discomfort and the change." Because you know that on the other side, a whole new world awaits. A world you yourself create, with empty pages in the book of your life story that you get to fill as you please. The power you gain from Reiki defies explanation, and once you remember your innate ability to heal yourself, that knowing stays with you for all of eternity.

When you learn something like Reiki, you want to keep it for yourself for a while. Play with it. Experience it. Make it your own. At least I did.

But eventually, you want the people around you to get to experience the same thing you have. Reiki is not for me alone; it's a gift that's meant to be shared, a blessing to be passed down from generation to generation, parent to child and friend to friend. Nothing compares to helping other people see their own magnificence.

I'm not saying that "Reiki has enlightened me!" or "My life is perfect now!" Far from it, I still struggle every day. But now I have a tool when I need one, spiritual guidance literally at my fingertips anytime I ask.

I have a daily meditation in the Reiki principles that takes less than one minute to do, yet still reminds me every day of what really matters. I have unlimited access to Universal Intelligence and the higher realms. I am infinitely more equipped to deal with the challenges that present themselves to me, trusting that whatever happens in my life, I can turn it into something good, great even.

If my stomach hurts, I can send myself Reiki. If I remember a painful moment from my past, I can send karma-clearing energetic frequencies back through time and space in that direction. No longer is my first thought to call a doctor and look outside myself for healing if I fall ill, for I know that the cure lies within.

"With great power comes great responsibility," said Voltaire. I have a responsibility to spread this ancient truth to as many people as I can. Every man, woman and child should know their power and have access to Reiki as far as I'm concerned. One look at all the global problems we face today, and the need for Reiki in these challenging times becomes very, very clear.

Besides, who knows how big an impact I can have and what the ripple effects may be? I myself will probably never know, for the great thing about books is that they aren't subject to the life and death cycles we humans must endure. The least I can do is throw the seeds of my knowledge to the wind and let the flowers bloom as they may.

That is why I wrote this book. For you. For you to understand what Reiki is and how you can use it to heal yourself and change your life. I wrote this book in the hope that Reiki helps you thrive and feel the happiness and peace that is your birthright. I want to inspire you to receive a Reiki attunement and join the Reiki community; who, by virtue of raising their own vibrations, are raising the collective vibration of our planet.

Enough of this nonsense of most people "living lives of quiet desperation and going to the grave with the song still in them." Those days are over. There is too much suffering in the world, and most of it, in the developed nations at least, we are inflicting upon ourselves with our own minds.

Rumi asked us why we choose to stay in prison, when the door is so wide open. Let's walk out that door now, using Reiki as the key to break the chains and limitations of our minds once and for all. We deserve to be happy. To know that we can connect to Spirit any time we want. To be truly free.

I hope that Reiki transforms your life as it has mine and that you fall in love with this sacred healing technique and build an eternal bond with it like I have. The world would be such a different place if everyone lived from their heart and felt free to express their unique energy in the world.

As the great Lao Tzu said, "Give a man a fish, and feed him for a day. Teach the man to fish, and feed him for a lifetime."

Here's to learning how to fish!

WHO THIS BOOK IS FOR

Being a universal force from Spirit, Reiki belongs to all who seek and desire to learn the art of healing. - Hawayo Takata

This book is for anyone who wants to learn more about Reiki. You may find yourself attracted to Reiki for any number of reasons. Maybe you want to learn an easy technique for deep relaxation and peace of mind, a simple way to stay calm and centered in this busy world of technological overwhelm. Or perhaps you are looking to increase your psychic abilities, help your loved ones or learn how to send energy to your dog or cat.

Even though those are all very legitimate reasons, regardless of why you think you want to learn Reiki, there is always something underlying that desire; a force pushing you forward, urging you to grow and get on with being your best self already.

It may start as a little thought in your mind, one you can easily push down and ignore with all the suppression techniques so readily available to us today: television, food, shopping, busyness, alcohol... etc.

Sooner or later, your dissatisfaction with the status quo grows. Even if you can't put your finger on it, you know something is missing. Surely you exist for a reason and have a greater purpose for being here. Even if you aren't consciously aware Reiki can help you find that meaning, your intuition understands Reiki can act as a bridge between where you are and where you want to be.

Reiki will connect you to your soul; to pure Source energy, Universal Intelligence, Great Spirit, God, whatever word you use. Yes, it will help you heal the pains and illnesses of your physical body. But it can do so much more. It can remind you about the divine spark inside of you and help you remember why you exist here on Earth in these exciting times.

If you want the ability to sit calmly amidst the chaos, to be so secure in your connection to all that is that you live each day happy and free, there is a profound and transformational tool that can help. If you are ready to awaken, heal and remember the truth of all you are, this book is your guide.

Please allow me to introduce you to the sacred Japanese healing technique of Reiki.

WHAT IS REIKI?

The secret art of inviting happiness... the spiritual medicine of all diseases. – Dr. Mikao Usui

If we break down the word *Reiki* into two parts, *Rei* and *ki*, *Rei* means *spiritually-directed* and *ki* means *universal life force energy.*

Together, they mean 'spiritually-directed universal life force energy'. Reiki is the energy all around us being specifically directed by the Great Spirit.

During a Reiki session, the Reiki practitioner becomes a channel for this spiritual force to flow through.

The practitioner acts like a vessel for the energy, almost like a pipe or a container to hold the spiritual vibrations and condense them so they can go wherever they are needed most. The Reiki may work on one specific area in your body or multiple areas at once to create a balanced whole.

The experience of having these frequencies flow through you connects you to the higher realms on a very deep level, which is why so many people consider Reiki to be a spiritual practice, one done in honor and respect of the soul.

That being said, Reiki is not a religion. There is no belief system attached to Reiki and people of all religions and faiths practice it. Some people even find that they become more religious after they take Reiki, since they experience their religion firsthand instead of merely having an intellectual concept of it before.

Reiki might start as a fun, little hobby, a side interest to pass the time. That is, until it changes you at your very core, revolutionizing your mind and awakening you to your true powers and ability to heal.

Then, you begin to see that Reiki is magic. With practice, you learn how to keep your feet firmly planted on the ground while your head stays in the clouds. You are able to bring down the wisdom and guidance of the spiritual realms into your everyday life, growing roots and wings at the same time.

Used correctly, this timeless method of healing will catapult you in the direction of the person you are destined to be.

> *I believe there exists One Supreme Being, the*
> *Absolute Infinite, a Dynamic Force that governs*
> *the world and Universe. It is an unseen spiritual*
> *power that vibrates, and all other powers fade into*
> *insignificance beside it. So therefore, it is Absolute!*
> *I shall call it 'Reiki'. - Hawayo Takata*

HOW REIKI WORKS

The visible world is the invisible organization of energy. - Physicist Heinz Pagels

Everything is energy

Learning about Reiki is really an education into how the world works. Everything in our Universe is made up of energy and emits a vibration out into the world. Denser objects, like pens, vibrate at a lower frequency; while living things, like people, possess life force and vibrate at a much faster rate.

The Japanese call this life force *ki*, the Chinese use the word *chi* and in India they refer to it as *prana*. Regardless of the name we give this force, it is our essence and what gives us life.

Every cell in our body, every organ and every thought we think is made up of this ki and has its own unique vibration. Even though most of us can't physically see energy with our eyes, (I say most because some people can!) it is always present nonetheless.

When our soul first inhabits our physical body in our mother's womb, we vibrate at the same frequency as Source. Our vibration is so fast, we simply cannot wait to be an actual person and experience life!

Inevitably, things happen in our life experience that create energetic blockages in our body and slow our vibration down. Our fourth grade teacher tells us we're not good at math, and we believe him. We get in a car accident and become deathly afraid to drive at night. Our heart gets broken for the first time, and instead of dealing with the pain, we push it down where it lives on as stuck energy in our heart chakra, which we then protect with a strong wall around it to prevent *that* from ever happening again.

Even external influences like cell phone and laptop emissions, environmental toxins and genetically-modified foods affect our vibration in a negative way.

By the time we are grown, we typically have more than a few of these energetic blocks preventing our energy from moving around freely inside our body. When the energy is stuck and has nowhere to go, it ends up creating issues in the nearby organs, muscles and tissues.

In comes Reiki to the rescue. All vibrations affect matter to some degree, and with Great Spirit directing the Reiki energy, its ability to influence matter becomes exponentially stronger. The Reiki enters our body and goes straight to the cause of the imbalance, dislodging any stuck, stagnant frequencies along the way, charging up the entire area with positivity, and clearing our meridians (energetic pathways) so the life force can flow easily again.

If we think of our body as a brook, the Reiki acts like a burst of fresh water barreling down it, pushing any rocks and debris aside and cleansing and purifying the stream along the way.

We know more than we think we do

On an intuitive level, our souls know and understand that all things vibrate. We've just been conditioned to forget. Even so, we still use phrases like "I get a bad vibe (vibration) from him" or "That really resonates with me" - which is just another way of saying "That thought frequency moves at the same rate as mine on the subject!"

Cultures around the world have used vibrational healing for thousands of years and we carry this understanding in our DNA. Percussion instruments - which people have used to drum on and harness the energy they emit - are among the oldest instruments known to man.

It may take a little while for you to think in terms of frequency and vibration, since you are basically learning a new language- one of energy. You probably won't be fluent overnight.

The concepts in energy medicine can sometimes feel abstract or hard to wrap our heads around, since they go against many things we've been taught our whole lives. We learned to focus on the tangible and that "seeing is believing," when in reality, we need to concentrate on what we cannot see in order to create what we can.

The most powerful healing tool we have is our mind

Our intention during a Reiki session is more important

than anything else. Since our thoughts carry a great deal of vibratory power, when we set our intention to be the channel for Spirit, we create that reality and become that channel.

With the power of our thoughts, we bring about that which we want to see in our life experience. Every second of our conscious lives, we are creating. The problem is, if we don't *consciously* create, we still create regardless, only we end up making what we don't want. But when we intend to be the channel during a Reiki session, we put our minds to work for us instead of against us.

> *If you realized how powerful your thoughts are, you would never think a negative thought again. - Peace Pilgrim, a woman who walked for 28 years across the United States to promote peace within herself, other people and our world.*

The trifecta of giver, receiver and Great Spirit

Reiki is a co-creation between the Reiki practitioner, the recipient and Spirit. Together, they form a perfect triangle, which is the shortest way for three distinct lines of energy to intersect and make a complete energetic circuit so vibrations can travel in a continuous loop.

Once we intend for the healing to take place, we let go of how, when or even if the healing will happen. We may ask for the Reiki heal a particular person, issue or situation, but ultimately the outcome is outside our control.

Our limited viewpoint prevents us from seeing the best way for things to unfold. From the bird's eye view of Infinite Intelligence, however, all things are known. The Reiki always works, just not necessarily in the way we think it should or according to our personal timeframe.

We are never the ones doing the healing, we are simply the containers to hold the light energy that does.

All healing is self-healing

So many people come to Reiki so they can "heal others," only to discover the real person they need to work on is themselves. This is good news, since the only person we can fix, change or heal is ourselves anyway.

Only when we accept this, as well as understand that we will likely be refining our vibration for the rest of our lives, will we ever be able to support others in their return to health.

You may have heard the idea that everyone around us is a mirror, reflecting parts of ourselves back to us. If we change, the reflection in the mirror must change as well. If we raise our vibration, we will attract higher frequency people and situations into our lives. Like attracts like.

With every person we practice Reiki on, we get a chance to heal something in ourselves. Since the Reiki flows through us on its way to the recipient, we receive a healing along the way. Hence the common saying in Reiki circles: "Give a treatment, get a treatment."

You can only heal with love

Since the only person we can heal is ourselves, even if we never send Reiki to another person, only to ourselves, that is more than enough. Our body's capacity to hold light energy will increase and other people will receive a healing just by virtue of being around us. They will pick up on the inner peace reflected in our aura, and every time they enter our field they will benefit from the peaceful vibrations emanating from us.

When we have such self-love that we accept all parts of ourselves, we show other people that it's okay to accept themselves as well. We lead by example, and spread self-acceptance through the energetic communications that take place behind the scenes. Although we might think that we need to take on other people's suffering and transmute it for them, only when we shine our light fully can we do our best work.

Maybe you've been around someone and felt a deep sense of calm or a joie de vivre that you just can't explain. You can be that person for someone else. Every time you expand your consciousness by practicing Reiki and choosing to emit higher quality frequencies from the radio signal that is your mind, your soul evolves. Since all of humanity is connected and we are all one people, as you rise, everyone else does too.

The only thing you need to ask yourself every day is, "What can I do to raise my vibration today?"

Ultimately, Reiki will work regardless of whether we understand how it does or not. We don't need to comprehend every intricate detail to still benefit from its effects.

Sometimes, Reiki will even work if a person doesn't consciously believe in it but their Higher Self accepts it and knows it to be true. As long as the person's soul doesn't block and reject the Reiki, it can still work its magic.

That's how I personally understand the mechanism behind Reiki, to tell you the truth. In my mind, it is a combination of two parts physics, one part mind power and one part pure magic.

> *If you want to find the secrets of the Universe,*
> *think in terms of energy, frequency and vibration. -*
> *Nikola Tesla*

THE BENEFITS OF REIKI

A comprehensive system of healing, Reiki affects us on multiple levels: physically, emotionally, mentally and spiritually. Both preventative and curative, Reiki helps us stay healthy while still targeting any issues we already have.

Reiki is able to work on such a deep level because Dr. Mikao Usui, the man who developed the system of Reiki we use today, understood that our body follows our mind and our mind follows our spirit.

First, we have an imbalance on the spiritual level. It then moves down to the mental level, permeating our thoughts and emotions, and if left untreated, will eventually manifest itself on the physical plane as pain, illness or disease.

Since the roots of all issues lie on the spiritual realm, Dr. Usui put our spiritual health above everything else. He had us connect to Spirit before every Reiki session so it can focus with laser-like precision on the core reasons underlying our problems. With that connection, not only do we reap the spiritual rewards from Reiki, we also get to enjoy the trickle-down mental, emotional and physical effects as well!

Regardless of whether you can use more mental clarity, help dealing with challenging emotions or relief from a physical problem, Reiki will give you the spiritual reboot you need. It works beyond our wildest dreams, often in ways we couldn't have even imagined, since the Reiki healing energy truly knows no bounds.

PHYSICAL BENEFITS OF REIKI

Physical pains and diseases heal faster.

Reiki has been known to help with a variety of issues, including:

- headaches and migraines

- cuts and bruises

- broken bones

- insomnia

- back pain

- colds, and

- cancer

Your body has a natural tendency to heal. Just look at

what happens when you get a cut. The surrounding tissue immediately rushes to the rescue to stop the bleeding and instantly starts to repair the area.

The human body is amazing in what it will do to bring itself back to balance and harmony. When your innate healing abilities join forces with Reiki, you get a double dose of healing and need less time to return to your original state of health and well-being.

Physical ailments can even disappear altogether.

My friend Jared is a beach volleyball player whose shoulder bothered him for years. After one Reiki treatment at a volleyball tournament by a Japanese woman, Jared hasn't had any pain in his shoulder since.

Now, Reiki doesn't always work like that. If you have had a physical issue for, say, thirty years, it's a bit unrealistic to expect that it will go away completely in a one-hour Reiki session. These miracles do happen, however, and stories like Jared's abound in the Reiki community.

Since physical issues always start elsewhere, their origins stemming from the suppressed emotions and spiritual discord of yesteryear, once Reiki addresses the original cause, the physical manifestations often go away. Pain is simply our body talking to us and telling us that something is wrong. If we listen and fix the underlying causes with the help of Reiki, our body has no need to continue the conversation.

We feel lighter and freer in our physical bodies.

Almost everyone has felt tension and stress in their neck and shoulders after a long day or stressful event. The expression that we "carry the weight of the world on our shoulders" is often not that far off from the truth!

Those knots we feel are just stuck energy, the issues in our tissues that result from pushing down our feelings and not feeling free to express them so they can leave our body. Reiki moves that energy out of our energy field. Once it does, we can feel like we've just shed twenty pounds overnight. We are designed to live healthy lives, free of illness and disease, and Reiki helps us remember that.

EMOTIONAL BENEFITS OF REIKI

We feel a deep sense of calm and peace.

Since Reiki induces what researchers call the Relaxation Response, which is a state of complete and utter peace, after a Reiki session you often feel like you couldn't think a negative thought if you tried.

Things (or people) that used to bother you no longer elicit the same charge. You've raised your vibration, so those lower frequencies will bounce off of you in their search for other frequencies vibrating at the same rate they are. Since you're no longer a vibrational match, they will often leave your experience altogether and you won't have to deal with them at all anymore!

We become balanced.

Reiki provides us with an unshakable balance and the reminder that we are centered and strong. If we are uncertain of our foothold, the slightest push or shove can knock us off-kilter. But with the steadiness that comes from a consistent Reiki practice, we can handle anything that comes our way. We will either take the blow and stay standing, or we will shift gears and deflect the hit altogether.

Reiki balances our chakras so our energetic centers can work together synergistically. It evens out the masculine and feminine energies in our bodies (both males and females have both) so we stay strong yet compassionate, intuitive while still taking action.

Our stress levels go down.

Time and time again, Reiki practitioners and clients report their stress melting away after a treatment. When we access our soul - that place where only truth exists and stress is but a by-product of incorrect thinking - we experience the joy that comes from simply being alive and we wonder why we were so frazzled and worried in the first place.

Anxiety and worry are common causes of insomnia and other sleep issues. Raúl, a seventy-year-old retired college professor who just learned Reiki this past year, had a hard time falling asleep his entire life. Now that he sends himself Reiki every night before going to bed, he falls asleep easily. "Reiki pretty much solved my problem," Raúl said. "I combine the Reiki hand positions with deep breathing and often fall asleep right in the middle of my self-treatment."

MENTAL BENEFITS OF REIKI

We get a break from the incessant chatter of our mind.

Reiki helps us slow down, and when we do our thought waves slow down as well. In an age where people get frustrated if a website takes longer than one second to load, Reiki forces us to put our extended concentration on one thing and one thing only: our present experience.

Even if we drift off during a session, chances are we are busy healing some memory deep in the recesses of our mind and are just getting the conscious part of our brain (the one in charge of any resistance) out of the way so the healing can take place.

We often feel exhausted after running around all day, even if that race has only been on a hamster wheel in our mind. The demands of a job, family obligations and modern-day living require us to constantly give our attention (aka our energy, aka our power) away to external forces. When that energy leaves our body, it also leaves our aura – the electromagnetic field surrounding us that protects and shields us. No wonder we can feel so drained!

There will always be one more email to send, one more phone call to make, one more task to check off our To-Do list. We will likely leave this planet with a list of things we always wanted to do but never quite got the chance.

When we slow down to practice Reiki, we also slow down our thoughts, which helps clear our minds. Free from their usual frenzied pace, our minds can then focus on personal growth and development and really getting to know internal world. Ironically, it is precisely when we allow ourselves to pause that we often move forward with great leaps and bounds.

We stop taking ourselves so seriously.

Reiki helps us remember that life is meant to be enjoyable. When we put our individual experiences into the bigger picture of our life, we realize that something that seems so important at the moment probably won't even matter five years from now.

If someone cuts me off, it could be the best thing that could happen because it prevents me from getting in an accident. If another person treats me poorly, I get a chance to practice standing up for myself and defining what I will and will not accept in a relationship.

Reiki helps us put our life in perspective. From that greater vantage point, we can see that above all, life is for the fun of it.

We receive answers to troubling questions.

If we have a big decision to make, we often go back and forth and ruminate about what will happen if we make the wrong choice. We try to think things through with logic and reasoning and pro and con lists.

Reiki offers us another way. We can either hem and haw over our dilemma, often losing sleep in the process, or we can just enter the meditative state of Reiki and let the answers come to us as clear as day. Even if they don't appear, the sense that everything will work out just fine regardless of what we decide often does.

Reiki offers us a great clarity that results from connecting with a higher source of wisdom than our own. The choice is ours: we can either grow quickly and easily, or slowly and painfully. The answers we seek are always available to us. All we have to do is listen.

SPIRITUAL BENEFITS OF REIKI

Our psychic abilities greatly increase.

Reiki often jumpstarts our psychic abilities, since being psychic is really just having such a strong connection to Spirit that we can tap into that all-knowing intelligence at any time.

Our mind is like an antenna that allows us to pick up external frequencies, including those from Spirit. Before a Reiki attunement, most people can only hear static. Once an attunement strengthens our connection, however, a tremendous amount of information often comes pouring in as clear as day. Many people become eerily psychic following an attunement, just knowing that someone was going to call or a certain event was going to happen.

In school, we are taught to use the analytical left side of our brains while our intuitive right side remains largely undeveloped. When it comes to psychic abilities, however, the more we can turn our rational thinking off, the better.

Reiki teaches us how to quiet our mind so we can hear messages and guidance from the Universe. When we connect to the place where all things are known, we are able to recognize the signs all around us and see truths that were previously hidden.

We evolve and grow, both as a human and a soul.

Reiki challenges our long-standing beliefs about ourselves and the world we live in. Old memories from our childhood will often rise to the surface to be dealt with and released for good.

In times of great trauma, pieces of our soul will often depart our body as a protection mechanism. Whatever is happening is simply too much for us to handle, so those soul fragments will leave to protect themselves from being destroyed. In the safe, sacred space of a Reiki treatment, however, many people experience a spontaneous soul retrieval and those bits and pieces return.

When those parts of our soul come back to us, we are able to patch ourselves back together; not as something broken, but as a whole that is even stronger than before, with more vibrancy and strength than we even knew we had.

We remember our reason for being here.

In a Reiki II class that I taught, within a few weeks of receiving their attunement, all four students quit their jobs.

Time and time again I have seen the invisible force of Reiki push people toward their personal destiny and their dreams. Once our spirit gets rejuvenated, coasting along just won't do. Instead, we want to do those things that make our soul shout, "Yes!"

A REIKI ATTUNEMENT

What is a Reiki attunement?

A Reiki attunement is a sacred ceremony between you, a Reiki Master and Spirit. The Reiki Master transfers pure Source energy from the ethers into your body.

As soon as you receive an attunement, you are dialed in to the exact frequency of Reiki and can channel this healing energy. If you were an electrical circuit, which in a sense you are, an attunement turns on the switch so you can be a conduit for the Reiki electricity to move through.

An attunement also initiates you into the Reiki lineage of all those who have come before so you can draw upon their wisdom and expertise.

During an attunement, which lasts about ten to fifteen minutes, you sit with your hands in prayer position and your eyes closed. The Reiki Master Teacher will often create sacred space and set the stage for this special ritual. I like to make a crystal grid surrounding the person, play Tibetan singing bowls and do a short, guided meditation beforehand.

There is nothing to do or think about during an attunement. You can simply be to be and just exist. That alone can be quite liberating!

How does an attunement feel?

During an attunement, light energy pours into your body. Many students find this to be a very powerful experience. Not every day that you encounter pure Source energy in such an intimate way.

The best way to go into an attunement is without any expectations. You may feel relaxed, sleepy, energized or absolutely nothing. Some students see colors, while others get glimpses of past lives or connect with loved ones who have come down to be part of the ceremony. Whatever you feel (or don't feel) is absolutely perfect. You can rest assured that the attunement worked and the ability to channel Reiki is now yours.

Tuning in to Source

The purpose of an attunement is to make you a better channel for the Reiki to flow through. To do this, the Reiki moves through your body for 21 days following your attunement, clearing away energetic blockages and obstructions so you can hold more light energy.

Unfortunately, the detoxification process isn't always fun! (Okay, it's never fun.) As the Reiki flushes out the lower energies from your body, you often experience them one last time as they are on their way out.

However, you always come out better on the other side. A healing crisis is a real blessing, even if it doesn't necessarily feel that way at the time. Your body is recalibrating and replacing old energies with more positive ones that reflect your true nature.

Once you receive an attunement, you always have the ability to send Reiki. Its imprint on your cellular makeup crosses lifetimes. If for whatever reason you decide not to use your Reiki for a while, it will simply lie dormant until you do.

A Reiki attunement can be a life-changing experience, a milestone after which you are never quite the same again. You become more *you*, which you soon discover is not such a bad thing to be.

A REIKI TREATMENT

No two Reiki sessions are alike. You have a different experience every time, since you are always a
different person with different energy than you were the
day before (or even an hour before.) Every Reiki treatment
is a once-in-a-lifetime chance to work with your energy
exactly as it is in that moment.

The most common reaction is to become deeply relaxed. Many people also feel heat from the practitioner's
hands, almost as if they were two small heating pads. Some
people laugh or talk, while others cry or fall asleep during
their session. People often say they feel like they are moving in and out of consciousness during a treatment.

A typical Reiki session consists of a person sitting or lying down in a comfortable environment, fully clothed, while a Reiki practitioner sends them the Reiki. Sessions usually last about an hour and the Reiki practitioner will either place their hands on or above the person's body.

Some practitioners use Reiki symbols - which represent a particular type of energy, like peace or power - to help direct the Reiki and enhance its effects. Other practitioners just like to be the channel for the Reiki and not use any symbols. Either way works just fine.

Since Dr. Usui wanted his system to be as simple as possible, he only put three steps into a Reiki treatment. First, the practitioner puts their hands together in prayer position at their heart to center and ground themselves. Next, they connect with Spirit and ask for the recipient's healing. The last step is the treatment itself.

A First Degree Reiki practitioner can give an in-person session, while a Second or Third Degree practitioner knows how to give a long-distance treatment. The first time I received a distance healing, I was a little skeptical. I didn't have high hopes and thought I probably wouldn't feel anything. But I was so wrong! The heat was so strong that it felt like a sun was shining down right on top of my stomach.

Reiki practitioners also give themselves self-treatments. People get together and practice Reiki in group settings as well and often call these gatherings Reiki shares. Group healings are especially nice because the more practitioners there are, the more energy they can hold and direct toward a specific end.

Reiki is becoming more and more mainstream as more people hear of its benefits. Over 800 hospitals in the United States today now offer Reiki, thanks to its effectiveness and how well it works alongside Western Medicine.

So, what does it feel like to experience Reiki? It's a bit difficult to describe since it defies logical explanation. Magical is the closest I've come.

But, why take my word for it? Why not get a Reiki treatment so you can form your own opinion? Or better yet, take a Reiki class so you can send Reiki to yourself!

THE REIKI SYMBOLS

The symbol for the word 'Reiki'

*There is a thinking in primordial images, in symbols
which are older than the historical man, which are inborn
in him from the earliest times, eternally living, outlasting
all generations, still making up the groundwork of the
human psyche. It is only possible to live the fullest life
when we are in harmony with these symbols; wisdom is a
return to them.*

- Carl Jung

The power of a symbol

For thousands of years, civilizations the world over have communicated through the use of symbols. Symbols offer explanations. They tell stories. We only have to look at cavemen drawings to see our natural tendency to use symbolism as a way to confer meaning.

However, the power of a Reiki symbol goes far beyond just being an image. A Reiki symbol is a holographic, three-dimensional representation of a particular healing frequency. There are many Reiki symbols out there, although Dr. Usui only used four or five. Subsequent Reiki Masters have added additional symbols into their teachings, some of which they received from great masters in Tibet while others they channeled directly from Spirit.

How the Reiki symbols work

When we use the Karma Clearing Symbol, for example, we invite the energy of karma clearing into the Reiki session. We turn our entire focus toward getting rid of unwanted karma. Our mind power acts like a magnifying glass on the symbol and intensifies the energy it represents. The symbol becomes a portal, a doorway through which we can access the full vibrational spectrum of karma clearing.

If we want to understand the full significance and potential of the Reiki symbols, we must first look at how our minds work. Our subconscious mind - that part of our brain that makes 95% (!) of all our decisions, usually without us even being aware it's doing so – "thinks" in symbols rather than words. Symbols are the language of the subconscious mind.

Since our subconscious mind will do whatever we tell it to, when we work with the Reiki symbols, we speak directly to it and command it to focus on certain energies. Let's say we hold a negative belief that money is hard to come by. Our subconscious takes that belief as truth and factors it into our decisions when it comes time to buy new clothes or go out to dinner.

But if we repeatedly hold the Reiki symbol for growth in our mind's eye and focus it toward our bank account, our subconscious will eventually start to believe that our funds are growing and money comes easily. When we give our subconscious mind new energies and beliefs to focus on, those 95% of our decisions end up looking very different.

One mind, one intent

Every time we call on a symbol, we also sync up with every Reiki practitioner who has ever used that symbol before. If we draw the Peace Symbol, we link our mind up with everyone else to vibrate one collective frequency of peace. We send massive waves of peaceful energy out into the world, infusing the Peace Symbol with even more of itself in the process.

The symbols work, too! One time, I was arguing with my mom and I mentally drew a huge Peace Symbol between us. Mid-sentence, my mom stopped talking and said, "And... and... and I forget what I was going to say!" She must have lost her train of thought after she subconsciously felt the Peace Symbol in her aura, which then sent a signal to her brain to think about peace.

You don't have to use the symbols with Reiki by any means, and many a successful Reiki treatment has been given using no symbols whatsoever. But the symbols offer a focused intent to our Reiki and connect us with higher levels of awareness. They vibrate our energetic pathways with their specific frequencies and also give our busy minds a single point to focus on. Not too shabby if you ask me.

The stone symbolized something permanent that can never be lost or dissolved, something eternal that men have compared to the mystical experience of God within one's Soul. - Carl Jung, referring to Stonehenge

THE HISTORY OF REIKI

Dr. Mikao Usui, the original Reiki Master

B efore we get into the origins and history of Reiki, let's think about what history really is for a second. It's his-story, or in other words, someone's interpretation of what happened in a previous time period.

But who's to say what truly happened during that time? Memory is a tricky thing, and even if we are talking about the same event with two people who were there, their stories will probably differ in a few key respects. History is always subjective. Show five people the same movie, and they'll each explain it a bit differently. As writer Anaïs Nin said, "We don't see things as they are, we see them as we are."

Imagine if someone tried to tell the story of your life a hundred years from now. Could they really capture your fears, desires and what moves you to get up each day? Or would their version just be a watered down, paltry explanation of your full existence?

I will share the key players in Reiki's history with you: Dr. Mikao Usui, Dr. Chujiro Hayashi and Madame Hawayo Takata. Thanks to Reiki Masters like Frank Arjava Petter and William Rand, who researched Reiki's history, we now have a more complete and accurate account of what happened.

Even so, uncovering the full truth is difficult, if not impossible. Madame Takata, the woman who brought Reiki to the Western world, changed bits and pieces of Reiki's history to make it more appealing to the Western palate. Japanese language can also be interpreted in many different ways and inherently allows each reader to derive their own meaning from it.

We will probably never know exactly what took place, and that's okay. At the very least we have a wonderful healing modality that works and continues to help us flourish, grow and heal.

Dr. Mikao Usui

The history of the Reiki system we use today begins with a man by the name of Dr. Mikao Usui. A lifelong student, Dr. Usui traveled extensively throughout China, India, Europe and the Americas, studying various healing arts and spiritual concepts like Chinese medicine, yogic philosophy and the art of divination.

In 1922, Usui Sensei climbed Mt. Kurama in Japan and meditated for 21 days. Some historians say he was searching for a way to do hands-on-healing that didn't require him to use his own personal energy, while others say he was seeking enlightenment and inner peace.

Regardless of his initial reason for climbing the mountain, after fasting and being with himself for 21 days, Usui Sensei felt a powerful beam of light go directly into his crown chakra, giving him the very first Reiki attunement- and a long-distance one, at that!

On his way down from Mt. Kurama, Usui Sensei stubbed his toe. When he put his hands over it, he felt energy emanating from them and his toe was healed. Excited by this, Dr. Usui started to practice and hone his newfound ability on himself and his family.

He started a healing group called the Usui Reiki Ryoho Gakkai and developed his own method of healing, which he called Usui Reiki Ryoho (Usui Reiki Healing Method). While other people in Japan were also doing hands-on-healing and Reiki at the time, Usui Sensei added in his extensive knowledge about healing and metaphysics to make his own comprehensive system.

Dr. Usui opened a Reiki clinic in Tokyo and began to offer treatments to anyone who asked. Word traveled quickly, and soon many people came to his clinic seeking healing and guidance.

After a large earthquake devastated Tokyo in 1923, killing more than 140,000 people and leaving thousands of others homeless, injured and emotionally scarred, Usui Sensei began to train people how to teach Reiki so they could then initiate more practitioners and help with the massive need. He also added the Reiki symbols and the attunement process to his system at that time.

In 1925, Usui Sensei opened up a second Reiki clinic and traveled all around Japan, teaching over 2,000 students and attuning 15-20 people to the Reiki Master Level. He died the following year of a stroke, leaving behind a legacy and a healing method for all to use.

Why we refer to him as Usui Sensei

In Japan, a Sensei is a teacher or person who has mastered an art form. The literal translation of Sensei means someone who has been "born before", a person who teaches from their own experience of their craft. Calling someone a Sensei is a way to show them honor and respect.

One of Dr. Usui's students wrote the inscription on his memorial, which reads: "Someone who works hard to improve body and mind to become a better person is called a man of Great Spirit. If he uses that Great Spirit for a social purpose to teach and improve society, he is a teacher. Usui Sensei was one such man."

Here is a person who helped countless others, a beautiful soul who was committed to sharing his knowledge and spreading his technique. A true Sensei indeed.

Dr. Chujiro Hayashi

Of the 15-20 students Usui Sensei attuned to the Master Level, the most well-known is Dr. Chujiro Hayashi. Not long before his death, Usui Sensei asked Dr. Hayashi, a retired naval officer and medical doctor, to open his own Reiki clinic in Tokyo and continue to develop Reiki there.

Hayashi Sensei opened his clinic and added his medical knowledge to the existing Usui Reiki system for the next thirteen years or so. Whereas Usui Sensei had taught students to intuitively scan a person's body to determine which areas to treat, Hayashi Sensei added hand positions to the sessions and took detailed notes about which hand positions worked best for which organs and conditions. By doing this, Hayashi Sensei added structure to Reiki and helped practitioners talk about this mystical practice in more tangible terms.

He also had people lie on a table and receive Reiki from multiple practitioners at once, while with Usui Sensei they sat in a chair and received a treatment from one practitioner only. Since the Reiki practitioners worked together in groups at Hayashi Sensei's clinic, their intentions could sync up into one collective consciousness and their separate flows of energy could all come together into one powerful and unified current of Reiki.

In 1937, Hayashi Sensei went to Hawaii with his daughter for several months to teach Reiki. A few years later, in the midst of World War II, the Japanese government asked him to share his knowledge of potential Hawaiian targets and locations.

A man of great peace, Hayashi Sensei refused to share this information with the Japanese government because he knew they would use it toward malicious ends. The Japanese government called him a traitor and a spy, and the only way for Hayashi Sensei not to disgrace his entire family was to perform a ritualistic Japanese suicide called seppuku. Hayashi Sensei made this ultimate sacrifice and died with honor in 1940.

Madame Hawayo Takata

In 1935, a Japanese-American woman from Hawaii named Hawayo Takata visited Hayashi Sensei's clinic in Japan for a number of severe issues, including asthma and anxiety. After two treatments a day over a four-month period, Takata Sensei had cured herself of her conditions. Awed by this, she stayed at the clinic for another year to learn Reiki before going back to Hawaii to practice.

When Hayashi Sensei went to Hawaii to teach two years later, he initiated Madame Takata to the Reiki Master Level and also asked to speak with her. A great war was imminent, he told her, and unless she continued the legacy of Reiki in the United States, the great tradition would be lost forever.

Sure enough, not long thereafter World War II began to rage and Dr. Hayashi's Reiki clinic in Japan was destroyed. When the United States occupied Japan at the end of World War II, it declared all Japanese healing arts illegal. Only Western medicine was allowed. Reiki went completely underground, only to be used in secret societies and amongst a select few.

Hawayo Takata continued to teach Reiki in Hawaii, attuning students to Levels I and II. She waited thirty years to attune students to the Master Level, and attuned her first Reiki Master in 1970. Twenty-two students became Reiki Masters under Takata Sensei, including her granddaughter Phyllis Furumoto, and Reiki spread far and wide from there. Were it not for Takata Sensei, Reiki would likely only be practiced in Japan to this day.

Now that we have the Internet and much easier access to historical information from around the world, we now know that Takata Sensei took some liberties with Reiki's history to make it more accessible to Americans.

She said that Mikao Usui was a Christian, when in reality he was likely a Buddhist or even more spiritual in nature than anything else.

Takata Sensei also created a different attunement for Reiki I, Reiki II and the Master Level, whereas Usui Sensei used the same attunement for all three levels. She explained that we must not teach Reiki for free, and put a $10,000 price tag on the Reiki Master attunement that had never been there before. However, maybe Takata Sensei did this because she knew American culture often determines the worth of something by how much it costs instead of its inherent value.

We also have to remember that Takata Sensei was teaching Reiki during and immediately after Pearl Harbor, World War II and the Japanese internment camps. The changes she made to the Usui Reiki system were almost certainly in response to and a reflection of the high anti-Japanese sentiments at the time.

Our Western Reiki Lineage

Dr. Mikao Usui started this amazing healing art form. He adapted the existing hands-on-healing techniques of his time, added the Reiki principles and symbols and gave us a compete system of healing to use. Usui Sensei focused on uniting body, mind and spirit, emphasized self-healing and taught over 2,000 people in a few years time. Those people in turn shared Reiki with their family and friends, and here we are, a hundred years later in countries all over the world, still using his technique.

Dr. Chujiro Hayashi gave us the hand positions and the power of group healing through one shared energy stream. He had the foresight to attune Hawayo Takata to the Master Level so Reiki would not stay contained in Japan, but rather explode as a healing force out into the world.

Madame Hawayo Takata took Reiki mainstream. She simplified the hand positions, unified the teachings and added order to an esoteric, intuitive art so more people could grasp it.

From each of their stories, one thing is abundantly clear: they all had the common desire to share this healing technique. They never wanted to amass the knowledge and simply keep it for themselves, but rather to use it and help others. The moment we receive our first Reiki attunement, we join a lineage filled with some great individuals indeed.

What we can take away from Reiki's scattered past

There are a number of different Reiki branches and traditions taught today. Almost all of them use a combination of Japanese and Western techniques, and ultimately the differences don't matter. There is but one Reiki, one spiritual source from which all is derived. To embody that spiritual energy as best as we can is our only finish line, and there are many roads that will take us there.

I actually like the discrepancies in the teachings, because they force us not to rely on what came before but to forge ahead and create our own path. Perhaps if we had one set way to practice Reiki and that was it, it would only encourage us to put someone else in charge of our healing, even if that person was Dr. Mikao Usui. The disjointed Reiki history makes each of us to create our own Reiki. In doing so, not only do we assist in its evolution, we progress right along with it.

Our gift

How lucky that we have this technique to draw upon during these times of great change and chaos, life and death, beauty and destruction and great awakening. We have a tool to keep us balanced and remind us what we're made of, a guide to not only help us stay afloat but perhaps even take flight.

We owe this blessing to those who came before us. Their beautiful legacy lives on in every attunement, every Reiki session and every time someone chants the Reiki principles. I have every faith that they continue to guide us from the spiritual realms, igniting the candle to bring light to the darkness and helping us see every step of the way.

THE FIVE REIKI PRINCIPLES

The secret way of inviting happiness, the spiritual medicine to cure all diseases.

Just for today,

> *Do not be angry.*
>
> *Do not worry.*
>
> *Be grateful.*
>
> *Do your work honestly.*
>
> *Be kind to every living thing.*

Every morning and evening, join your hands in prayer. Pray these words to your heart, and chant these words with your mouth. Usui Reiki Treatment for the improvement of body and mind.
- The founder, Mikao Usui

How the five Reiki principles began

A few years after Mikao Usui opened his first Reiki center in Kyoto, he began to realize something. People would come to the clinic and see results from their Reiki treatments, but they would inevitably come back not long thereafter complaining of the same problem or issue.

Usui Sensei wanted his system to provide lasting health and well-being to people, not a quick band-aid fix that relieved them of their symptoms but never offered a cure.

He realized that real healing requires us to work with our minds as well as our physical body. Mind, body and spirit are all interconnected. Our thoughts cause our emotions; which, if left unexpressed, then manifest on this physical plane. In other words, our thoughts create our physical reality.

If we focus only on body and spirit but leave our mind out of the equation, we can never create lasting change. Usui Sensei wanted to show people how to think so their physical issues would never resurface again.

We are going to emancipate ourselves from mental
slavery, because while others might free the body,
none but ourselves can free the mind. – Marcus
Garvey

We must commit to the growth of our soul

Usui Sensei also wanted us to understand that we play a crucial role in our own healing. If we want a Reiki treatment to have a lasting effect, we must have a sincere desire to keep improving and bettering ourselves. We must commit to our growth and be willing to delve into the root causes of our physical issues, however painful and uncomfortable they might be to look at. Essentially, we need to accept responsibility for our own healing. No one can heal ourselves but us.

Usui Sensei wanted to add something to his method of healing and spiritual development that would help us think more constructively and that we could turn to for support.

Enter the five Reiki principles.

How to work with the five Reiki principles

Usui Sensei admired the Japanese emperor at the

time, Emperor Meiji, and based his Reiki principles on the moral guidelines the emperor gave to the Japanese people.

Dr. Usui recommended that we chant the five principles, which are called the Gokai in Japanese, twice a day, once in the morning when we wake up and again at night before we go to sleep. These are two very powerful times, because our energy reconnects with Spirit when we're asleep and our conscious mind takes a backseat while our subconscious mind runs the show. Right before we enter the dream state or as we return from it, the line between our physical dimension and the spiritual realm tends to blur.

Usui Sensei recommended putting our hands in prayer position, called gassho position in Japanese, while we chant the Gokai. As our hands come together, we balance the left and right hemispheres of our brain and prepare our minds to internalize the wisdom of the principles.

First we "pray these words to our heart," and then we "chant these words with our mouth." When we say the words aloud, we vibrate our entire body from the inside out with the sound of our voice. We move our internal energy with the words we speak, hitting all our meridians, chakras and organs along the way.

Word sound has great power. When we chant the Gokai, every cell of our being is vibrating to the exact frequency of what we are saying. Far more than just words, the Gokai is a mantra, a statement that directs our mind and takes it precisely where we want it to go.

How to meditate on the Gokai:

With your hands in prayer position, recite the Gokai in the morning and again at night.

First, mentally chant the words as you focus on your heart center. Then, speak them aloud.

The depth and power behind the Reiki principles

Deceptively simple, each principle is an extremely profound, complex spiritual concept reduced down to a simple sentence.

Japanese written language is subjective in nature and leaves a lot up to our personal interpretation of the characters. To me, that means we can each find our own meaning in the principles and incorporate them into our lives in ways that work for us.

Were we to embody these five ideals each and every day, not only would be Reiki practitioners, we would *be* Reiki and radiate this healing energy everywhere we went.

"Just for today" or "Today only"

How powerful that the Gokai begins with the words "Just for today" and that Usui Sensei incorporated the Buddhist belief that the time is always now into his guidelines.

The future hasn't happened yet and the past is just a matter of interpretation. When we approach our lives with this one-day-at-a-time philosophy, we break healing down into more manageable pieces. I probably won't be able to abide by the first Reiki principle and never get angry again in my entire life. However, if I commit to letting go of any anger and refuse to let it hold me back just for today, that seems much more doable.

Let us begin now with the first Reiki principle:

Just for today, do not be angry.

THE FIRST REIKI PRINCIPLE:

DO NOT BE ANGRY

Do not be angry (Ikaruna)

We begin with the first rule of thumb of the Gokai: *Do not be angry.*

Since we want to use the principles in ways that make sense to us personally, I turn this first principle into an affirmation and say *Just for today, I let go of anger and feel peace.*

I remove the word 'don't' from the principle, since I'm fascinated with how our brains comprehend language and many scientists in the field of neurolinguistics believe our brains cannot process words like 'don't' and 'no'. Our subconscious mind literally ignores these words. For example, if I tell you, "Don't think of a purple elephant," what is the first thing you think of?

Ideally, I would love to develop my internal thought processes to the point where I can avoid getting angry in the first place. But I'm just not there yet.

Truth is, sometimes I *am* angry. If I tell myself, "Do not be angry," not only does that not ring true for me, I'd probably get mad at myself just for saying that! *Don't tell me what to do and not to be angry, if I want to be angry I'll be angry!*

But if you prefer the original translation, use it! You want to apply Reiki to your life in your own way. Personalize it. Make it yours. Combine your unique vibration with its elevated frequency to create a healing art that is your very own.

Just for today, I let go of anger and feel peace.

Let's first look at the three usual targets of our anger: a situation, another person or ourselves. Every time we experience this uncomfortable – and very human – emotion of anger or any of its close cousins (rage, fury, resentment,) we are almost always sending our anger in one of those directions.

Anger at a situation

When something happens outside our control - like we lose our job, get broken up with or someone we love gets sick – we can easily get angry because we feel helpless to change the situation. Why did this horrible thing happen to us and why didn't we have any say in the matter?

As hard as circumstances may be, they always give us the opportunity to grow and become stronger. As Napoleon Hill, the author of one of my favorite books *Think and Grow Rich* said, "Every adversity, every failure and every heartache carries with it the seed of an equivalent or greater benefit."

Even if we practice our Reiki diligently, we will still experience sorrow and grief; that's just part of being human. But as one of Usui Sensei's influences, Buddha himself, said, "Pain is inevitable. Suffering is optional." We can only control our response to painful events and not the events themselves.

If we teach our brains to respond differently to unfavorable circumstances, we can reduce our suffering tremendously. We can literally "change our minds" and learn to catch ourselves as soon as we start to feel angry. Instead of allowing that anger to smolder inside of us, we can get it out, use it for transformative purposes, or at the very least reflect on what we can learn from it.

Instead of automatically moving into a victim mentality and thinking *This horrible thing happened to me*, with practice we can shift our perception and think *Okay, this happened, but it's a chance for me to grow. Some good will come from this, even if I don't quite know what it is yet.* Even if the only gift we glean from the situation is that we can now help someone down the road with the same issue, there are always life lessons to be learned and soul growth to be had.

Anger at another person

> *Holding on to anger is like drinking poison and*
> *waiting for the other person to die. – Malachy*
> *McCourt*

In Chinese medicine, the organ associated with anger

is the liver. If we hold on to anger, we injure our liver and make it harder for it to perform its functions, which can result in various problems ranging from sleep and weight issues to anxiety, depression and even breast cancer.

Being angry with someone has actually been one of my biggest hurdles to overcome. My father left when I was two and I never heard from him after that. I kept all my anger toward him shoved down so far deep inside, I didn't even realize it was there!

After I began my journey with Reiki, the detoxification process that happened afterward brought all my anger up. I was *mad* for an entire year. Furious, even. All the rage I had suppressed my whole life came rushing to the surface.

But over time, I realized that being angry with my father didn't change anything. It got me no closer to fixing the abandonment issues I had, and only kept me stuck in victim mode, thinking someone else did something to me and *It's all his fault.*

While my anger and blame relieved me of having to do anything to change the situation, they also robbed me of my power to fix it. My father held the power over my emotions instead of their rightful owner – me.

Where our attention goes, our energy flows. By directing all my mind power and thoughts toward being angry, I was actually strengthening that feeling and perpetuating the situation. What we focus on expands.

One thing that helped me manage my anger tremendously is the reminder that people do the best they can with the resources they have at the time. Just like they say you can't judge a man until you've walked in his shoes, I have no idea what life was like for my father when he left or the unique set of experiences that made him who he is.

Although my father's actions hurt me, his behavior had nothing to do with me and was just a reflection of what was going on inside of him. By working with myself to really understand and internalize that, I was able to set myself free.

Forgiveness is a gift we give ourselves

Forgiving someone does not mean you condone what they did. Instead, it just means you refuse to let their actions impact your life for one more second.

Nor does forgiving someone mean you have to have a relationship with that person. About four years ago, I looked for my half-brothers and sisters on my father's side and talked to my father on the phone for the first time. We communicated for a few months, but little by little I realized that doing so wasn't good for me and I'm better off not having him in my life. Fortunately, I can still reap the benefits of forgiveness while maintaining a healthy boundary in that relationship.

Anger is a secondary emotion

While on the outside I was mad at my father for leaving, underneath there was a great deal of hurt and sadness the anger was covering up. There is almost always a root emotion behind our anger. After my first Reiki attunement, yes, I was furious for an entire year, but I cried every single day the next.

It was a process, for sure, but I got to work on trust and abandonment issues that have likely plagued me for lifetimes. Now that I've dealt with a lot of them, I feel so much lighter. I let go of a ton of weight and created space for positive qualities and new experiences to come in.

Anger at ourselves

Of course, there's that anger that's often the most harmful of all, the anger we turn toward ourselves.

Why did I do that? Why didn't I do that? How could I have been so stupid? We're often the hardest on ourselves, holding ourselves up to these impossibly high standards of perfection before we even have a chance to make the necessary mistakes that show us the way. We can even berate ourselves for straying off-course, when not only have we never been to the destination, we've never even seen a map.

I've even gotten angry with myself for being angry! *Why can't you just let this anger go? Seriously? You're going to be mad when you know no good can come from this?*

We would often never dream of talking to another person the way we talk to ourselves. If we can forgive other people's mistakes and understand they are only human, perhaps we can extend that same courtesy to ourselves.

So go easy on the person you are. The mere fact that you are reading a book about Reiki shows you're interested in improving your life and becoming more yourself. That says a lot in my book (which this is).

The transformative power of anger

Anger isn't necessarily negative in and of itself. When we're the angriest can often be when we are the most motivated to change our current situation. The fury ignites a powerful fire within us that we can either use as a creative or a destructive force. It can push us toward creating positive changes in our lives or it can destroy us completely. The choice is ours.

Ways to manage our anger

Anger does the most damage when left unexamined. If we ignore rage or pretend it's not there, it just grows inside us and eventually has no choice but to express itself in a physical way.

Ideally, we want to acknowledge our anger as it arises and commit to getting it out as soon as we can. There are lots of ways to release anger... you can go beat a pillow senseless, take a kickboxing class or scream at the top of your lungs in your car (hopefully with the windows rolled up!) I went to the batting cages every single week during the Year I Was Furious.

You can write a letter, rip it up and throw it in the trash as you visualize your anger being thrown away right along with it. You can remind yourself that letting go of anger brings peace, and that ruminating over what someone else did – no matter how egregious – will never get you where you want to go. You can picture a stop sign in your head and think *STOP* every time you catch yourself starting to get angry.

You probably won't be able to let go of your anger every time. But the first time you set the intention to do so, you will create a little groove in your brain. Every time you have the same intention after that, the groove will get a little deeper. Once you intend to let the anger go enough times, eventually your brain will automatically go there the next time you get mad.

Anger stems from wishing the past could have been any different. But all we can do is work with where we are now. In doing so, we create our future. How liberating to say, "I forgive everyone for everything" and truly mean it!

We can't direct the wind, but we can adjust our sails. – Bertha Calloway

THE SECOND REIKI PRINCIPLE:

DO NOT WORRY

Do not worry (Shin pai suna)

Usui Sensei understood that the great happiness thief of worry not only robs us of the present moment, it can even create the very thing we're worried about.

But, how does that work? you might ask. *Didn't you just say in the previous chapter that we're not in control of what happens to us? That Universal Intelligence and forces beyond our control are pulling the strings? Be consistent here, Brookie.*

I understand the confusion, but there are greater forces at play that exist alongside our massive ability to create - the two are not mutually exclusive.

Usui Sensei wanted us to focus on the part of the equation we can control – our thoughts. He understood that our thoughts create our emotions and our emotions create our reality. When we worry, we are visualizing and setting into motion the opposite of what we want. So he advised us in the second Reiki principle to trust that every situation in our lives is happening in perfect timing and for a reason.

Just like with the first principle, I modify this second principle and take the word 'don't' out of it so my subconscious mind doesn't get confused. Besides, who knows how Mikao Usui would have worded his principles if he had the access to neurolinguistics that we do today?

I change this principle to *Just for today, I trust in the Universe*. But, again, do what's right for you. (Just in case the five hundred thousand times I've said that already haven't been enough.)

Just for today, I trust in the Universe.

Working with this second principle has really helped me have faith in the grand scheme of things. If I want a particular outcome, I use the Reiki Manifestation Symbol and send Reiki to it. After that, I have to let it go and leave it up to the Universe. I've done everything I can.

Let's say you want a particular job. You may want this job so badly and send Reiki to the situation every chance you get, but if it's not in your best interest to get the job, you won't get it. Your Higher Self and Universal Intelligence know what experiences your soul needs much better than your mind does. Your limited human vision may not be able to see that a job a thousand times better suited to you is waiting right around the corner.

This second Reiki principle helps us live in surrender and acceptance. We do everything we can to add our input to the creative process, and then we get out of the way for things to happen as they must.

> *Don't you worry 'bout a thing... 'cause I'll be standing by your side when you check it out... – Stevie Wonder*

Ways to stop worrying
- Remind yourself that worrying is negative goal-set-ting and can actually backfire and create the very thing you're trying to avoid.

- Make a Worry Box out of a shoebox. Every time a worry shows up, write it down on a piece of paper and put it in the box. Once in the box, that worry is out of your hands, both literally and figuratively.

- Unplug your computer, phone and electronics from time to time. Disconnect from the physical world so you can reconnect with Spirit. Seeing what other people are doing on social media can invite comparison and encourage us to worry that we're not where we should be in life. But, most people only show a mask to the world. They keep their innermost challenges and fears to themselves, and we end up comparing our troubles to someone else's false pretense of perfection. Doesn't sound like a very fair comparison to me! Give yourself time to tune out so you can tune in to the realm of truth where worries don't exist.

- Focus on what you want. If you're worried about how you're going to pay your bills this month, instead of giving energy to that, see yourself paying them easily and with money to spare. Picture that scenario over and over in your mind. It may feel unnatural at first, but with time it will get easier. Olympic athletes

DO NOT WORRY   91

visualize every detail of their race or swim and see themselves standing on the pedestal wearing that gold medal, so know you're in good company!

Go easy on yourself when you worry anyway

You're human, and our natural human tendency is to use our negative mind first. Back in the day when we were running from wild lions and tigers, we had to be cautious; it helped ensure our survival. Even though we no longer need to think that way, our brains haven't quite caught up to the 21st century.

The next time you have a scary thought, understand that it's part of being a person and then let it go as best you can. See it float on by like a cloud in the sky. If you have trouble releasing your worries at first, have compassion for yourself. The last thing you need is to be worried that you're worried! It takes a lot of emotion behind a worry to bring it to fruition. The very fact that you're aware of your anxiety and are actively working to let it go is probably enough to prevent it from happening.

We are such powerful beings, the writers of our own stories. The more we can stay unattached to the outcomes of our creations and just create for the sake of doing so, the better. After that, que será será.

What if it didn't matter what happened next?

THE THIRD REIKI PRINCIPLE:

BE GRATEFUL

Be grateful (Kan sha shite)

This third principle reminds us to be thankful for what we have at this moment. Not what we want in the future or hope to have one day, but what is showing up in our current experience as we speak.

When we can see the beauty of what we have, we create even more things we can be grateful for. A vibration attracts other similar vibrations. The Law of Attraction is a Universal Law, which means it is a truth that exists in the Universe all the time.

If I think about how grateful I am for my dog Bamboo, my next thought will be how thankful I am for my dog

Jazzy too. Which leads to me thinking about how happy I am that I got to take them on a walk this morning while so many people sat in cubicles at jobs they want to leave but haven't quite figured out how to (yet). Next thing you know, I'm feeling so lucky that I've created a life for myself where I get to empower people by introducing them to Reiki while still having enough money to buy organic, local food (aka medicine) from the Farmer's Market. Which makes me thank my lucky stars for persimmons, asparagus and Persian cucumbers... and on and on it goes, my high frequency of gratitude attracting similarly high frequencies of gratitude to me.

Every day, we can either make a brightly-colored kaleidoscope of thoughts with our mind or an expanding loop of negativity. These thoughts of ours have infinite creative power. Let's use them wisely.

A couple ways to bring more gratitude into your life

1. After you say the five Reiki principles each day, write down five things you are thankful for. Commit to finding the diamond in the rough, even if you have to search like mad!

Okay, so I hurt my knee inner tubing. (True story, by the way.) *Now, I get to write that book I've wanted to write* (the one you're reading now) *which I probably would have continued to put off otherwise.*

By turning the situation around - all in my mind, mind you - I replace a woe-is-me attitude for hurting my knee with positive thoughts of taking inspired action.

2. Close your eyes, and take a few deep breaths. As you breathe in, mentally say, *I am*, and as you breathe out, *grateful*.

There is beauty in everything

When we train ourselves to see the gift in everything, we even learn to be thankful for the difficult moments that come our way. They force us to show our true colors, to share our talents and to help benefit mankind.

Today at least, we are *here*. We are *alive* and have one more chance to start anew. Not everyone gets this chance, and one day we won't have it either. But today we do, and for that I am grateful.

What are you grateful for?

THE FOURTH REIKI PRINCIPLE:

DO YOUR WORK HONESTLY

Tell me, what is it you plan to do with your one wild and precious life? - Mary Oliver

Do your work honestly (Gyo o hagame)

W e can translate this fourth principle into English in a few different ways. I've heard, *Do your duties fully*, *Walk diligently* and *Work hard*.

In my practice, I turn this principle into an affirmation and say, *Just for today, I do my work honestly.*

What is our 'work'?

Our work is not necessarily what pays for the roof

over our head or puts food on our table. It *can* be, if we align our thinking with that of Universal Intelligence. But if we are new to energywork and are still figuring some things out, there may be a bit of a time lapse between doing our work and making a living from it.

Our work is our mission, the reason we incarnated on this planet at this particular point in time and space. It's what our soul set out to accomplish during its temporary stay in our body. Our work is our purpose, our destiny. We all have one, even if it's buried down so deep in our unconscious that we have no idea what it is yet.

If you're one of those uncertain people, that's perfectly okay. Maybe you don't even need to know and never will. We live in the Great Mystery after all. Maybe the full significance of your existence won't be revealed until light years from now, long after you've left your physical body. It could be that one smile you gave that woman on the street that one day, which sparked an idea in her head that ultimately stopped global warming.

A great way to connect with your inner wisdom and your Higher Self - who knows full well what your work is - is to meditate on the five principles. Having a spiritual practice like Reiki helps you get away from searching for the answer and instead allowing it to present itself.

Your work certainly involves raising your vibration, and one of the best ways to do that is to do something you love, something that fuels your passion and stokes the flame within. Any time you get so engrossed in an activity that you lose track of time, your energy increases and so does its vibrational rate. In that moment, anyone would be hard-pressed to argue that you aren't doing your work honestly.

Wasting time doing something you love is not wasting time. – Paulo Coelho

Actually doing your work

Even when you know what your work is, sometimes actually *doing* it is another thing altogether.

Take me, for example. Part of the reason I'm here is to experience life and then write about it. To do that, I need to be willing to put myself out there for all to see, because that is where my soul growth lies. So does that

DO YOUR WORK HONESTLY   101

mean I sit down happily at my computer every morning and just let the words flow?

Um... not exactly. I will go to ridiculous lengths that amaze even me to do anything but. There are no limits to what I will do to get out of writing. *Oh, that's right, I just ate the last pomegranate seeds for breakfast. Better go to the Farmer's Market and get more, no way am I going one morning without pomegranate seeds!*

But eventually I sit down and I write, because that's the only way I can sleep in peace at night. Some days I don't make it there and that's okay too. Because when I do, and the words just come, there's nothing else I'd rather be doing. Even if I have to go through the whole rigmarole tomorrow, at least for today I got past the resistance.

We just have to do the best we can.

What does it mean to do your work 'honestly'?

The only person we have to be honest with is ourselves. That means forgetting about what society or our parents or anyone else expects of us. We only need to impress ourselves and be truthful about whether or not something is working in our life.

If we are really happy in that job or relationship, great! But if not, what is the smallest step we can take to point ourselves in a better direction?

> *Oh, just do what you want. Who cares what*
> *anybody else says. – Papa Davidson*

Pain equals no gain

Doing the work of our soul doesn't have to be painful. In fact, one could argue that if we are in pain we're not doing our work.

I'm not talking about a little blood, sweat and tears along the way. Our work won't necessarily be easy. But it should feel good and take us down a road we want to be on. When our life is over, our work will have been made up of those little things we did each day. As long as we did them with integrity and courage, what more can anyone ask?

> *If it feels good, you probably like it. If it doesn't, you*
> *probably don't. In your road to self-realization, it*
> *helps if you do what you like. – Alta*

THE FIFTH REIKI PRINCIPLE:

104 REIKI FOR BEGINNERS

BE KIND TO OTHERS

*Three things in human life are important. The first
is to be kind. The second is to be kind. The third is to
be kind. - Mother Teresa*

Be kind to others (Hito ni shinshetsu ni)

Usui Sensei considered this last Reiki principle to
be the most important of them all, and said that
sending Reiki to others is an excellent way to show them
kindness.

I learned to chant this principle as *Just for today, I
am kind to every living thing.* While that statement is oh-
so powerful, it is also perhaps the most challenging of all
the five ideals. Because to be kind to every living thing

means to treat *everyone* with the utmost respect and honor, including that person who can tend to get lost by the wayside sometimes – ourselves.

Many people get into Reiki because they want to help others. But if they give, give, give to everyone else but themselves, not only does their ability to send Reiki suffer, they suffer as well.

Being kind to yourself means not doing a Reiki session if you feel tired. It means having small self-care rituals that you do throughout your day to stay happy and at the top of your game. For example, you want to drink enough water (which flushes lower energies from your body,) move enough (which keeps your energy flowing) and get enough sleep (which is when you merge back with Spirit.)

Compassion all around

Confucius told us to "be kind, for everyone we meet is fighting a tough battle." We are all here to learn our own life lessons, and we have no way of knowing what those are for other people.

Sometimes our most challenging relationships can even show us how we don't want to be. Let's say someone we love isn't acting how we think they should. Perhaps they are eating too much and now have diabetes.

Our loved one is giving us a clear example of what can happen when a person lacks self-love and doesn't see their body as the temple it is. As bystanders, we are able to see the negative effects of eating too much without actually having to overeat ourselves. Our loved one may be suffering to show us that we don't have to, and we can choose a different path.

Being kind to every living thing also includes the planet we live on, which is very much alive, as well as the animals we share it with. Perhaps the kindest thing we can possibly do is offer our complete acceptance to everyone and everything, exactly as they are, without trying to change a thing.

Be kind whenever possible. It is always possible. - the Dalai Lama

FIVE WAYS TO INTEGRATE THE REIKI PRINCIPLES INTO YOUR EVERYDAY LIFE

1. Commit to chanting the Reiki principles twice a day.

You may have to make a note to remind yourself in the beginning, but if you meditate on the Gokai every day, it will soon become a habit. Nowadays, I automatically chant the Gokai without thinking as soon as I wake up. With very little effort on my part, I've been able to work with the principles on a very deep level just by making them a part of my daily routine.

2. Focus on one principle at a time.

When we concentrate on too many things at the same time, we scatter our energy and divide it up so no one energy stream can be particularly strong. If we focus on all five principles, each one gets 20% of our attention. But if we only work on the second principle, *Do not worry*, it receives the full 100%.

If my sole goal today is to trust in the divine order of things, I can catch myself more easily at the first sign of worry and remind myself, *Nope, not today, Brooke Betts. Today you trust that the Universe has everything under control.*

3. Focus on all five principles together.

You can also use the principles in conjunction with one another. Letting go of anger is an act of kindness toward yourself. Doing your work honestly may require you to take a leap of faith and trust that you will be okay financially. You may find that it is in the integration of the five principles that their full power lies.

4. Say the principles in both English and Japanese.

Some days, the principles mean more to me when

I say them in Japanese. Chanting them in their original language reminds me of the rich history of this spiritual practice I feel so lucky to be a part of. Usui Sensei chose the wording carefully to create a powerful rhythm and cadence. Besides, I imagine something inevitably gets lost in the translation.

But other days, I prefer the English version. When I say the principles in my native tongue, my brain can process each principle's meaning much more easily.

These are the affirmations I use:

Just for today...

> *I let go of anger and feel peace.*
> *I trust in the Universe.*
> *I am grateful.*
> *I do my work honestly.*
> *I am kind to every living thing.*

5. Put the five Reiki principles in places you will see throughout the day.

Tape the Gokai to your refrigerator, your mirror, the inside of your car, anywhere you will see them as you go about your day.

Not that I want to advocate using your cell phone any more than you have to - that thing may very well be the main cause of the decline of real human interaction in our world – but you can also create reminders of the principles on your phone and have them go off throughout the day. If you set your ringtone to a soft sound like a Tibetan singing bowl, you might be pleasantly surprised to hear the tone and read something like, *Trust in the Universe and know that everything happens at the perfect time.*

Essentially, you want to work with the principles in any way that will help their full meaning sink into your subconscious.

What if you were truly free from the weight of anger? If you trusted completely in the natural order of things, had deep gratitude for all that you have, lived a life full of meaning and purpose and showed kindness and love to everyone you met? I can only imagine how amazing that would feel!

THE THREE LEVELS OF REIKI

There are three degrees in Reiki: Reiki I (First Teaching), Reiki II (Inner Teaching) and the Master Level (Mystery Teaching). Reiki I works primarily on your physical body, Reiki II focuses on your mind and the Master Level works to advance your spiritual growth.

Reiki I - Shoden (First Teaching)

A Reiki I attunement opens you up physically so you can be a better channel for the healing energy. Some Reiki Master Teachers attune students to symbols in Reiki I, while others wait until the Second Degree and just place the symbols in the student's aura in a Level One attunement.

Because we have such a need for Reiki at this time in our evolutionary consciousness, I personally attune students to three symbols in the First Level: the Peace Symbol, the Power Symbol and the Centering + Grounding Symbol.

In a typical Reiki I class, you learn:

• any symbols the teacher attunes you to as well as how and when to use them

• the traditional hand positions for practicing Reiki on yourself and others

• how to give a complete Reiki session, and

• the origins of Reiki and the five Reiki principles

I also cover Animal Reiki in Reiki I when students are interested, and I would say they've been interested, oh, about 100% of the time.

After Reiki I, you determine when (and if) you feel ready to move on to the next level. Some students don't skip a beat and go right on to the next degree, while others like to marinate on what they've learned for a while.

Although most students wait until they take the

Second and Third Levels before opening up their own Reiki practice, after Reiki I you are a Reiki practitioner with all the tools to start your own private practice if you so desire. I know many Reiki I practitioners who are very, very powerful.

Reiki II – Okuden (Inner Teaching)

While a Reiki I attunement focuses mainly on your body, a Reiki II attunement works on your mind, clearing out old thought patterns and emotional blockages. It benefits your subtle, energetic body and offers you a deeper exploration of how your brain works. Since illness and disease start from seeds in your mind, unless you plant new seeds, the same weeds will continue to grow.

You also learn how to give a long-distance Reiki session through time and space, which allows you to send healing energy back into the past and forward into the future as well as anywhere in the Universe.

I have heard that we open up about twenty percent as a vessel for Reiki in the First Degree and the remaining eighty percent in the Second Degree. While I believe we all have our own unique experience, every Reiki II student

I've taught has said they felt a marked increase in their abilities after the second attunement.

In Reiki II, you receive the Mental + Emotional Symbol and the Distance Healing Symbol as well as any other symbols the Reiki Master attunes you to. I attune students to eleven symbols in the Second Level, including two symbols that clear karma, the Manifestation Symbol and the Heart Healing Symbol. We also explore the chakras in great detail and work with using pendulums in our Reiki practice.

The Master Level – Shinpiden (Mystery Teaching)

A Master Level attunement works on your spirit, preparing you not only to become a stronger channel but also to teach about the Great Mystery and attune others.

Usui Sensei broke the Master Level down into two parts: Assistant Teacher and Teacher. Although we live in a society that emphasizes instant gratification and having whatever we want "immediately if not sooner!" we can learn great lessons from assisting an expert and being an apprentice of sorts. We can develop skills that only come from taking our time to internalize this healing art form,

and our learning can skyrocket when we have the necessary space to reflect on what we've learned.

I teach about thirty-three additional symbols in the
Master Class, including three versions of the Reiki Master
Symbol and a few others that change our DNA and cellular
makeup. You also learn how to heal your ancestral lineage
and any issues from your past lives, which often results in
them disappearing from your current life.

Some people take the Reiki Master Course so they
can teach Reiki, while others take the class for their own
personal growth. When you become a Reiki Master, you
accept a responsibility to use your Reiki to help change the
world. Whether you do that through teaching or another
way matters not, as long as you stay true to your heart.

ADDITIONAL HEALING TOOLS

Reiki is a complete system of natural healing unto itself, one that unites mind, body and soul. Apart from receiving an attunement and holding the intention to use your Reiki for the highest good of all concerned, nothing else is necessary.

Some people like to keep Reiki separate and not "mix medicine", as my Lakota friend says. I personally love to combine other healing modalities and techniques into my Reiki practice, but it's a personal decision and either way works just fine.

I draw on my knowledge of the chakras and Five Element Theory in Chinese medicine. I share personal experiences and any intuitive hits I receive, as well as any messages from animal guides or the seven directions that add their energetic input to the session. I make crystal grids under the Reiki table, draw oracle cards before the session to guide me and include meditations, vocal toning and breath work if appropriate.

To me, these additions are like accessories to an outfit, and adding them to a Reiki session often takes it from nice and relaxing to a life-changing, mind-blowing experience never to be forgotten.

My three favorite accoutrements to Reiki are sound healing, crystals and other forms of energywork.

Sound healing

Everything in the entire Universe is made up of sound and has its own frequency. Technically, all energy-work, including Reiki, is sound healing because they all use sound and vibrations to affect and move matter.

We can manipulate ki intentionally with music, instruments, and let's not forget the most powerful sound healing tool known to man - our voice. When I do a Reiki session, I play music without words in the background to help induce a trance-like state for both me and the person on the table. I often use healing instruments like Tibetan singing bowls, a water drum with a deep base tone that mimics our heartbeat and a gong. Yogi Bhajan, a master of Kundalini Yoga, said that we can only resist the sound of the gong for ninety seconds. After that, our energetic body has no choice but to submit to its healing vibrations.

Crystals

Every living thing contains life force energy, and crystals, which grow on the Earth as well as deep below its surface, are no exception. Not only do crystals have ancient knowledge coded inside them, they are excellent for transmitting information and frequencies, which is why scientists and engineers put quartz crystals in watches, computers and other electronics to help broadcast energy.

Different crystals have different properties. Some carry positive energy that radiates outward, while others are great for protection or absorbing lower vibrations. You can place crystals on your body, carry them in your pocket and wear them as jewelry or a protective talisman.

You can also put a crystal grid formation under your Reiki table to create a matrix for energy to flow through. The crystals will sync up and pass information to one another, creating a pinball machine effect as the energy bounces from one gemstone to another. Use your intuition to decide which stones can help with the session and how to arrange them.

Fun fact: Crystals continue to grow even after they've been removed from the Earth. Unfortunately, the pace is so slow we can't see it in a single lifetime.

Fun fact #2: Many people believe Sedona, AZ lies on top of a giant crystal grid. After having lived there for a while, I'm a believer.

Other forms of energywork

Reiki works synergistically with other healing systems like polarity, shamanic practices, craniosacral therapy, Ho'oponopono (a Hawaiian method of healing) and acupuncture. Many massage therapists and psychotherapists use Reiki in their work as well.

120 REIKI FOR BEGINNERS

You may have knowledge of ancient healing arts you're not even aware of that you could use alongside your Reiki. A few weeks after my first Reiki attunement, I found myself putting my mouth about six inches above my dog Jazzy and sucking energy out of him before blowing it down to the Earth to be transmuted. I wasn't doing it consciously and honestly I thought I was a little crazy every time I did it.

Not until I told a powerful energyworker what I was doing did it made any sense to me. Very nonchalantly, he said, "Oh, yeah, that's a common technique Peruvian shamans do to remove unwanted energies. It's called *chupar.*" Apparently, I had this skill within my DNA the whole time and just needed Reiki to help bring it out!

One Reiki student was very visual and could actually see energy moving throughout the meridians and around the organs inside people's bodies.

Another student channeled someone's grandma the very first time we practiced Reiki. "You're a medium!" I said to her afterward. "What's a medium?" she asked. She had never even heard of the word before. Imagine how powerful she will be five years from now as she continues to develop her mediumship skills alongside her Reiki.

A medium, just in case you don't know, is a person whose body becomes a channel for a discarnate spirit to communicate information through. Essentially, we are all mediums for the Reiki energy every time we turn our Reiki on!

Since we are all connected to Source, every one of us has these extrasensory abilities and talents. Some come naturally because we've used them in past lives, while others we can develop and cultivate with conscious effort and practice.

You can also take your Reiki to the next level with:

- Pendulums

- Animal totems

- Color therapy

- Oracle cards

- Yogic breathing

- Aromatherapy and essential oils

- Massage, and

- Bach flower essences

Most new Reiki practitioners tend to copy the style of their teacher. As they gain experience and build their confidence, however, they start to develop their own style and create their own hybrid system of healing.

We all have skills we can add into our Reiki sessions, even if they are qualities we take for granted - like being a great listener or someone people feel safe to open up to. There is only one you. Your unique expression of life force energy will never happen in quite the same way ever again. Luckily, your only job here on Earth is to express it.

What ancient knowledge and talents lie dormant inside of you?

FINAL THOUGHTS

The most beautiful thing we can experience is the mystical. It is the source of all true art and science.
- Albert Einstein

If you're reading this, you probably have access to a computer or a smart phone. You are part of the elite twenty percent of the world's population that lives in an industrialized society and has access to first world comforts. You aren't frantic about where your next meal will come from, or your safety, or where you'll sleep tonight.

I say this not to diminish our problems because they indeed feel very real to us. Instead, I want to show that we are the lucky ones, those chosen few who have the means to effect real change in the world. We have a responsibility to all those people who don't, who are in survival mode and can't afford to think about developing their spirituality or mastering their thoughts.

Not only do they not have the time and luxury to focus on their inner selves, they usually don't have access to this information or even know it exists. We are so lucky that we do.

However, we need to heal ourselves first. As flight attendants always say when they explain the emergency guidelines before a flight, we need to put on our own oxygen masks first before helping anyone else.

We have so much power, and yet we often squander it away on worrying about what other people think, or what will happen if we fail, or how we can prove to everyone else that we're enough. We run fast and furious from our feelings, when in fact if we just allowed ourselves to sit with them, they could transform our lives.

This life is so sacred, not to mention short. It's a flash in the pan in the big scheme of things. How exhausting to wear a mask to the world when our spirit longs to be free, when we crave authentic self-expression and alignment with our soul. Reiki helps take off that mask. It brings us into the present moment and reminds us that all we have to do while we're here is evolve and enjoy this experience as best we can.

Is Reiki a magic pill? I wish. Yes, it feels amazing when the pure light energy of Reiki moves through us. But that light shines on our darkness as well, and shows us those places we've kept hidden for so long. We then have to put in the work and feel those emotions so we can release those lower energies once and for all.

It's not easy, but we must do it anyway. Because it's worth it. There is nothing like the peace, freedom and joy we get to feel when we live from our hearts.

Besides, we don't really have a choice. We must wake up if we are to survive this planetary shift that is moving us into higher levels of consciousness.

The Mayans understood the cycles of our solar system very clearly and knew we entered a new cycle on December 21, 2012. Since then, we have been in a transitionary period that marks the beginning of an era where we grow as a people and become more unified in our collective consciousness. The Kundalini yogis knew we were entering a new age as well, and that we will inevitably experience growing pains and moments of instability as both the light and the darkness are intensified at this time.

Now more than ever, we need tools like Reiki to help us manage our energy and keep up with the ever-changing state of affairs on Planet Earth. We need a way to stay steady among the energetic chaos we are constantly bombarded with.

The people in underdeveloped nations are relying on us to work through our own "stuff" so we can stop wasting our infinite energy/power (as the two are indeed interchangeable) and instead use our collective awareness as a force for good.

No more can we pretend that we are not all connected and each a unique spark of the same universal life force. When another suffers, so do we. When someone makes the effort to better themselves, we all benefit as well.

Every human being deserves health and happiness, and Reiki is an excellent road to get us there, an easy way to revamp our minds and change our brain chemistry. Your own personal Reiki practice can be nothing short of magical. An awakening to your true power. Self-healing at its finest.

There are some things that cannot be explained or read about in a book. You can read a thousand books on how to drive a car, but not until you get in one and actually do the darn thing will you learn how to drive.

That's how it is with Reiki. You might understand it on an intellectual level by reading about it, but only when you receive a Reiki attunement and experience it firsthand will you know it in your bones.

Once you use Reiki and see that it actually works (!), you realize that you can manipulate energy and use it toward creative ends. False beliefs like, *Well, that's just the way things are* can no longer stand up in the courtroom of your mind anymore. You know better. You've experienced otherwise.

Giving yourself the gift of a Reiki I attunement may very well be one of the best things you ever do for yourself. It certainly was for me.

Why wait? You can design a life that feeds your soul, one that you're excited to wake up to each day and live on your terms. The time is now to unlock your true potential. You already have the key/ki. Now you just have to learn how to use it.

We are all stars, every last one of us, and stars are meant to shine. Let's.

> *Education is the most powerful weapon we have to change the world. - Nelson Mandela*

THANK YOU

Thank you for allowing me to share this information about Reiki with you. Writing about this magical practice that has improved my life in so many ways only reinforces all that Reiki means to me.

Please thank yourself for taking the time to learn about Reiki and expand your consciousness as well. So many people want to live a life that's more in tune with their true nature, but how many actually take action to make that happen? You did, and you deserve recognition for that.

It is my deepest wish that you use Reiki to love yourself and see the truth of all that you are, as well as help others along their journeys.

For myself

Well, that doesn't sound egotistical at all, does it, dedicating a book to myself?

But if I am to practice what I preach - that all healing is self-healing, and that you can only heal with love, and self-love, at that - who better to give my dedication to than her?

So I dedicate this book to Brooke Cherie Betts, that person I get to wake up and be every day. Never again will she exist in quite the same way, I might as well appreciate her while she's here.

Even though she often stumbles, sometimes hides and can have a tendency to forget, her determination to look fear in the eye, her dedication to the evolution of her soul, and her desire above all else to be *free* from the shackles of her mind, what can I say... it gets me every time.

I love you and I got you, soul girl, forever and always.

ACKNOWLEDGEMENTS

Thank you Grandma and Grandpa for helping me so very much in so many ways. Thank you Mom for your constant love and support, even if this Reiki and healing business is completely foreign to you and you have no idea what I'm talking about half the time. I love you.

Thank you Vanessa Maynard for your beautiful cover and interior layout design, Amy Harshbarger for your excellent editing, Ravi Kumar and Julie Hinton for all your help formatting and Julian Wysocki for your wonderful pencil sketch of Dr. Mikao Usui.

Made in the USA
San Bernardino, CA
15 July 2016